LAUGH OUT LOUD
FARM ANIMALS

WENDY PIRK

iThink Books

Q. What do you call a grumpy cow?

A. Moo-dy.

Cattle

People have been raising cattle for at least 10,000 years. Modern cattle came from aurochs, a type of huge wild cow that lived in parts of Europe, Asia and northern Africa. The auroch is now extinct.

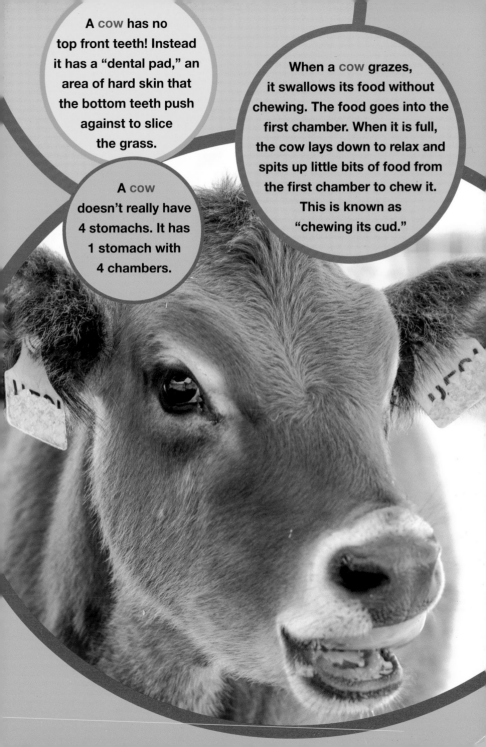

A cow has no top front teeth! Instead it has a "dental pad," an area of hard skin that the bottom teeth push against to slice the grass.

When a cow grazes, it swallows its food without chewing. The food goes into the first chamber. When it is full, the cow lays down to relax and spits up little bits of food from the first chamber to chew it. This is known as "chewing its cud."

A cow doesn't really have 4 stomachs. It has 1 stomach with 4 chambers.

Angus cattle can be black or red.

Texas Longhorns are descended from cattle brought to North America by Christopher Columbus.

Hereford cattle are known for their white faces.

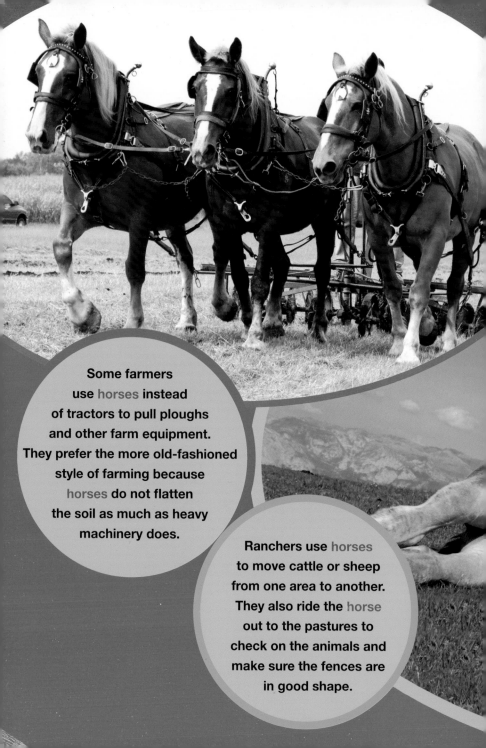

Some farmers use horses instead of tractors to pull ploughs and other farm equipment. They prefer the more old-fashioned style of farming because horses do not flatten the soil as much as heavy machinery does.

Ranchers use horses to move cattle or sheep from one area to another. They also ride the horse out to the pastures to check on the animals and make sure the fences are in good shape.

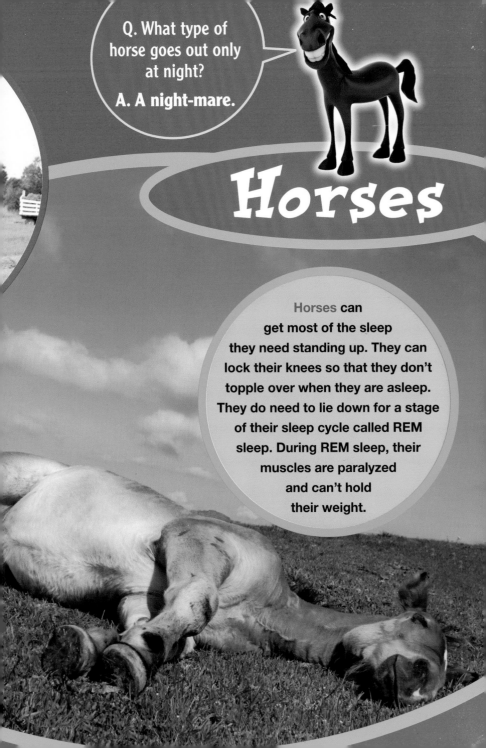

Q. What type of horse goes out only at night?

A. A night-mare.

Horses

Horses can get most of the sleep they need standing up. They can lock their knees so that they don't topple over when they are asleep. They do need to lie down for a stage of their sleep cycle called REM sleep. During REM sleep, their muscles are paralyzed and can't hold their weight.

What is the difference between a horse and pony?

Horses have longer necks and look thinner and sleeker. Ponies are stockier, like someone smooshed a horse to make it short and thicker.

Ponies are stronger than horses. A pony can pull twice its weight. A horse can pull only half its weight.

Horses and ponies are measured in "hands." Each hand is 4 inches (10 cm), about the breadth of a man's hand. Horses are usually 14.2 hands or taller at the withers (where the neck touches the shoulder).

Ponies are usually less than 14.2 hands high. There are breeds of mini horses that are pony-sized.

Ponies have thicker coats, so they can handle cold weather better than horses can.

Q. Why did the pony cough?

A. Because he was a little hoarse.

Pigs are smart, at least as smart as dogs. They can be trained to do tricks or walk on a leash. In some countries pigs are used to sniff out special mushrooms called truffles. In other places, they sniff out land mines, keeping people safe.

Pigs are great swimmers!

Sheep

Farmers raise sheep for their meat, milk and wool.

Sheep milk is higher in calcium than cow's milk. It is used to make certain types of cheese, yogurt and ice cream.

Some towns and cities use flocks of sheep to keep the grass short and the weeds down in parks and public spaces. Sheep are grazers and will eat the grass and weeds but not the trees or bushes. They are much better for the environment than lawn mowers or poisonous sprays.

Q. What is a sheep's favourite sport?

A. Baa-dminton.

Before

Wild sheep shed their wool every year, but most domestic sheep do not. If it is not cut, the wool will just keep growing.

If their wool grows for too long, sheep get really uncomfortable. The wool can get dirty and full of bugs, so the sheep get itchy. The wool also gets really thick, which makes it hard for the sheep to move around.

If the wool gets too thick, the sheep can get too hot and die.

Q. What did the well-mannered sheep say to her friend at the gate?

A. After ewe.

After

Most farmers shear their sheep in late spring so they will be cool in summer. This also gives the sheep enough time to grow more wool in time for winter.

Goats

Many farmers raise goats for their milk. Goat milk is easier to digest than cow's milk; sometimes when people can't drink cow's milk, they drink goat's milk instead.

Goat milk is also used to make many types of cheese. The flavour of the milk changes depending on what the goat eats. Cheese made of milk from goats that were fed different foods will not taste the same.

Some breeds of goat are raised for their fleece. Cashmere is made from the undercoat of cashmere goats. The fine hairs need to be brushed off the goat, not sheared like a sheep. It takes the hair from 2 to 4 goats to make 1 sweater.

Q. Why is it hard to chat with a goat?

A. They are always butting in.

Goats have rectangular pupils. They can look almost all the way around their bodies while they are grazing to watch for predators. They have only a small blind spot right behind them.

Many people think that goats will eat anything, but that's not true. Goats are foragers, like deer, not grazers, like sheep. They like trees and shrubs better than grass.

Goats are very curious and will nibble anything that catches their eye to see what it is.

Donkeys came from the African wild ass. African wild asses are endangered in their habitat.

Donkeys were bred to help people pull or carry heavy loads.

Today some farmers use donkeys instead of dogs to protect their sheep, goats and cows.

Donkeys make the best guard animals when they grow up as part of the herd or flock of animals they are going to protect. If an adult donkey is put into a flock or herd, it might fight with the other members instead of protecting them.

Q. Why don't you see donkeys playing hide-and-seek?

A. Because they are really good at hiding!

Donkeys **don't like dogs. They will chase foxes, coyotes and stray dogs away from the pasture. Some** donkeys **have even chased away bobcats and black bears.**

When a donkey **sees a predator, it brays and charges. This is often enough to scare the other animal away. If not, the** donkey **will kick at the predator with its front or back legs and may try to bite.**

Mules

A mule is the offspring of a female horse that mated with a male donkey. It is usually smaller than a horse but bigger than a donkey.

Q. What did the mule say to the blade of grass?

A. Nice gnawing you.

A female donkey doesn't often mate with a male horse, but when it does, the foal is called a "hinny." A hinny looks like a horse with long ears.

A **mule** makes a sound that starts off like a donkey's hee-haw but ends with a horse's whinny.

Mules are popular farm animals because they are stronger and can carry more weight than horses. They also have fewer problems with their legs and hooves.

Llamas

The **llama** was domesticated in the Andes from guanacos and vicunas. It was traditionally used as a pack animal and for its meat.

Q. What did the llama say when he was asked to take out the garbage?

A. No prob-llama!

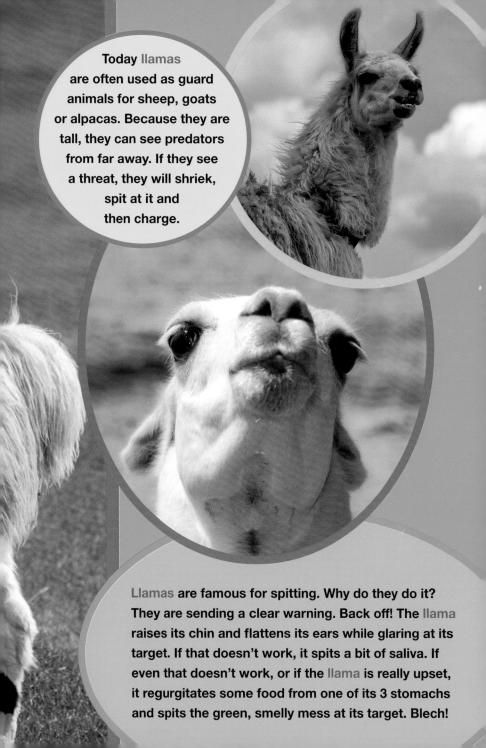

Today llamas are often used as guard animals for sheep, goats or alpacas. Because they are tall, they can see predators from far away. If they see a threat, they will shriek, spit at it and then charge.

Llamas are famous for spitting. Why do they do it? They are sending a clear warning. Back off! The llama raises its chin and flattens its ears while glaring at its target. If that doesn't work, it spits a bit of saliva. If even that doesn't work, or if the llama is really upset, it regurgitates some food from one of its 3 stomachs and spits the green, smelly mess at its target. Blech!

The alpaca is a close cousin of the llama. It is raised for its fleece, which is super soft, warm and water resistant.

Alpacas

It is easy to tell an alpaca from a llama. Alpacas are much smaller than llamas. They have short, spear-shaped ears while llamas have long ears shaped like bananas. Alpacas also have shorter snouts and are often fluffier, especially on the head.

Q. What did the alpaca say when he was invited to a picnic?

A. Sure! Alpaca lunch!

A herd of alpacas chooses a spot in their yard for a "poop pile," and every animal goes to the bathroom in that spot. Their poo, known as alpaca "beans," is often packaged and sold as fertilizer.

Alpacas do not make good guard animals because they are so shy.

Bison

About 200 years ago, as many as 500 million bison lived free on the plains of North America. Less than 100 years later there were fewer than 1000. If a few farmers hadn't started rising bison on their farms, the species might have gone extinct.

Most of the bison that are raised on farms and ranches are plains bison.

There are two kinds of bison: plains and woodland. Plains bison are smaller and used to range from the central prairies in Canada south to Mexico. Woodland bison ranged from the central Canadian plains north into the Northwest Territories, Yukon and Alaska.

Elk

Elk live wild in many areas of North America, but they are also raised on farms. Elk are part of the deer family.

One of the main reasons elk are farmed is for their velvet antler. Male elk shed their antlers every spring and grow a new set. When the new antlers first grow, they are made of cartilage, the same stuff that your nose is made from. Once they finish growing, the antlers harden into bone. Velvet antler is antler that is still made of cartilage. It is used in natural medicines.

Q. Why did the elk cry at the funeral?

A. He lost a deer friend.

Deer farms are not as common as elk farms. Some provinces in Canada do not allow deer farming because they are afraid that the farm deer will mix with wild deer.

One of the most common types of deer raised on farms is the white-tailed deer. White-tailed deer also live in the wild in many areas of North America.

Deer

Reindeer

Reindeer and caribou are the same species, but reindeer were domesticated in the Arctic areas of Europe and Asia sometime between 7000 and 2000 years ago. No one is sure exactly when. Caribou have not been domesticated.

Reindeer were brought to North America from Siberia around 1890.

In Europe and Asia, reindeer herders used their animals for meat, milk and fur. The reindeer were also trained to pull heavy loads.

Q. Which of Santa's reindeer has bad manners?

A. "Rude"-olph!

On reindeer farms in Canada and the U.S., many reindeer are raised to be show animals. People rent them for use in winter festivals, parades and other tourist activities like reindeer sleigh rides.

Q. What do you call a yak that can break up concrete?

A. A yak-hammer!

Yak farms are not common in Canada or the U.S., but some farmers are choosing yaks over cows because yaks are easier to care for.

Yaks are originally from the Himalayas, so they are used to cold, snowy weather. They can handle cold winters better than cows can.

Yak

Yaks **are
also known as
Tibetan bison or
"grunting ox."**

Camel

Most people don't think of camels as farm animals, but they can be. Camel farming is not common in North America but it is in other countries, like Australia and Dubai.

Camels are raised for their meat and milk. Camel milk is thought to be a very healthy drink. It is also made into many products like powdered milk, milkshakes, ice cream, chocolate, lip balm, skin cream and soap.

Q. What do you get if you cross a camel with a cow?

A. A lumpy milkshake!

There are 2 types of camels: Arabian camels, also called dromedaries, and Bactrian camels. Arabian camels have only 1 hump, and Bactrian camels have 2.

Camels have 3 eyelids and 2 sets of eyelashes. This protects their eyes from blowing sand in the deserts of Asia and Africa, where they originally came from.

On farms, dogs are not just pets. They are working dogs.

Guard dogs, like the Great Pyrenees, protect the farmer's livestock (cows, sheep, goats) from predators. These dogs are usually raised with the herd they are going to protect so they see the other animals as part of their pack.

Dogs

Q. Why didn't the dog want to play soccer?

A. It was a boxer!

Herding dogs move the livestock from one area to another. They also keep the herd together, making sure no animals stray too far away. Border collies are one of the best herding dogs.

Cats

Q. What is a cat's favourite song?

A. Three blind mice.

Cats were first used as pets in ancient Egypt. The Egyptians liked having the cats around to keep away any mice and rats trying to steal their grain.

Farm cats today have the same job.

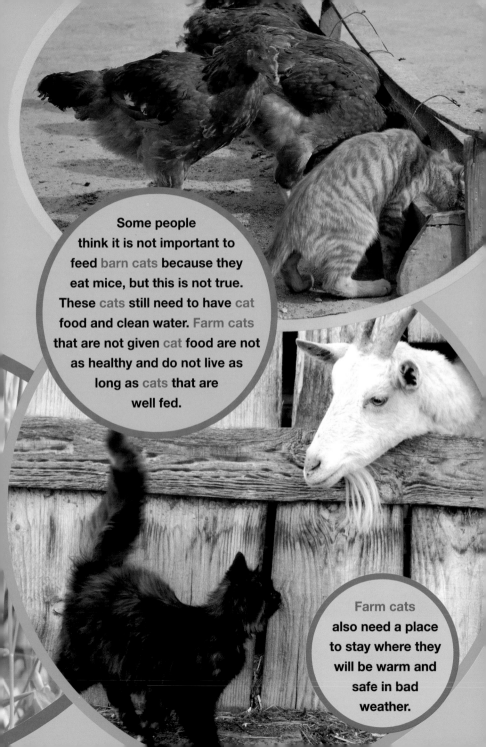

Some people think it is not important to feed barn cats because they eat mice, but this is not true. These cats still need to have cat food and clean water. Farm cats that are not given cat food are not as healthy and do not live as long as cats that are well fed.

Farm cats also need a place to stay where they will be warm and safe in bad weather.

Because we usually see them eating grain we tend to think chickens are herbivores. They are actually omnivores. They will eat bugs, small lizards, frogs and even mice.

Chickens

Turkeys were domesticated from wild turkeys that are native to North America.

Q. Why did the baby turkey bolt down his food?

A. He was a little gobbler.

The red dangly skin on a turkey's face above its beak is called a "snood." The skin under the beak is a "wattle."

Today many domestic turkeys have white feathers.

Male turkeys have sharp spurs on each leg that they use for fighting.

Turkeys

Ducks

Q. What do you get if you cross ducks with fireworks?

A. Firequackers!

Ducks are raised raised for down, eggs, meat or as show ducks. Some people also keep them as pets.

One of the most common ducks raised on farms is the American Pekin. duck.

Like most kinds of domestic duck, the Pekin comes from the mallard. Some Pekins even have the curved tail feathers the male mallard is known for.

Ducklings are precocial, meaning that they can get up, walk around and feed themselves soon after they hatch. The mom leads them to water, but they find their own food.

Geese are raised for their down, meat and eggs. Geese don't lay eggs as often as chickens do, but the eggs are much bigger. A single goose egg is equal to 3 chicken eggs.

Geese make great guard animals. They will honk loudly when they see a stranger or anything out of place.

Geese

Emu

The emu originally came from Australia. It is that country's biggest bird.

Q. Why did the emu cross the road?

A. To prove he wasn't chicken.

In the wild, the male emu is the one that incubates the eggs and raises the chicks. He sits on the eggs for 8 weeks before they hatch. During this time, he does not eat, and he gets off the eggs only a few times a day to turn them.

Emus are raised for their meat, eggs, feathers and oil. Emu oil is used in soaps, shampoos and skin creams.

Ostrich

The ostrich is the biggest bird in the world. It is originally from Africa.

It also lays the biggest egg in the world. An ostrich egg is 24 times bigger than a chicken's egg and about 2000 times bigger than a hummingbird's egg.

Ostriches are raised for their meat, feathers and eggs.

Some farms raise "game birds" that people like to hunt. One of the most popular game birds is the northern bobwhite. You can tell a female bobwhite from a male by the colour of its throat and eyebrow stripe. The female's are tan and the male's are white.

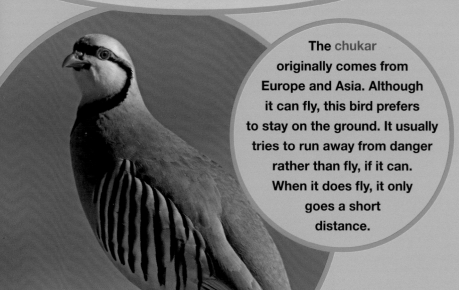

The chukar originally comes from Europe and Asia. Although it can fly, this bird prefers to stay on the ground. It usually tries to run away from danger rather than fly, if it can. When it does fly, it only goes a short distance.

Game Birds

Q. Why couldn't anyone see the birds?

A. Because they were in da skies (disguise)!

The ring-necked pheasant is another favorite game bird. It was brought to North America from Asia about 150 years ago. This bird spends most of its time on the ground. Special muscles in its breast let the pheasant burst into the air, flying almost straight up off the ground, to escape predators.

Bees

An average bee will make about 1/12 of a teaspoon of honey in its lifetime.

Bees gather pollen for food. A bee can gather pollen from 50 to 100 flowers before it has to return to the hive. A busy bee can visit more than 1800 flowers per day.

Q. What do bees do with their honey?

A. They cell it.

Beekeepers wear special clothes to protect themselves from getting stung.

On a bee farm, bees build their hives in special boxes. The beekeeper pulls frames out of the box to collect the honey. The real name for a bee farm is an apiary.

Salmon farms are big open-net cages in the ocean where salmon are raised.

Salmon

The Publisher: iThink Books

Library and Archives Canada Cataloguing in Publication

Pirk, Wendy, 1973–, author
    Laugh out loud: farm animals / Wendy Pirk.

ISBN 978-1-897206-19-5 (softcover), 978-1-897206-20-8 (epub)

    1. Livestock—Juvenile humor. 2. Livestock—Miscellanea—Juvenile literature. 3. Canadian wit and humor (English)—Juvenile literature. 4. Wit and humor, Juvenile. I. Title. II. Title: Farm animals.

PN6231.A5P57 2018   jC818'.602   C2017-906357-X

Front cover credits: Buffy1982/Thinkstock.

Back cover credits: Grigorev_Vladimir/Thinkstock; Maria Aloisi/Thinkstock; mcrosno/Thinkstock.

Photo credits: Every effort has been made to accurately credit the sources of photographs and illustrations. Any errors or omissions should be reported directly to the publisher for correction in future editions. *From Thinkstock:* acceptfoto, 48; anderm, 24; averess, 61a; BackyardProduction, 13b; Betty4240, 18b, 33a; BlazenImages, 29a; Calinat, 14; CarbonBrain, 32; CarGe, 28; castenoid, 8; ChiccoDodi, 22; clearviewstock, 55a; cowgirlrightup, 23; DanielPrudek, 39; DarcyMaulsby, 44a; darios, 61b; dgphotography, 5c; Dmitry_Chulov, 36; ejkrouse, 42; fotofrankyat, 45b; FoxyLadyDesign21, 40; giannimarchetti, 57b; Grafissimo, 27b; gregvandeleest, 63; GriffinGillespie, 31; Grigorev_Vladimir, 10; heckepics, 51b; HeikeKampe, 52; herbertlewald, 57a; Iteachphoto, 5b; jcrader, 35b; jeanro, 30; JoeGough, 8; johan10, 27a; JudyDillon, 16; JZHunt, 29b; KAdams66, 17b; Karl Weatherly, 26; KateLeigh, 43a&b; LeeTorrens, 62; lizzy-lou, 15b; Lynn_Bystrom, 5a; MaglidoPhotography, 53; Maria Aloisi, 20; Mats Tooming, 15a; Maxime Shebeko, 37; mcrosno, 3; Mirko_Rosenau, 50; Mr-Lonyly, 45a; Murgs001, 54; Neslo, 44b; OSTILL, 21a; Pavol Klimek, 60; pelooyen, 13a; photographybyJHWilliams, 58b; photosbyjim, 6; prabhjits, 38; purestock, 46b; RachelKathrynGiles, 55b; Rehlik, 49; Rena-Marie, 51a; RenePi, 4b; saja tawalbeh, 47b; SamanWeeratunga, 47a; Serge-Kazakov, 18a; shalamov, 11b; SherryL18, 11a; sickysick, 12; smiak, 59; Sparty1711, 33b; SteveOehlenschlager, 9, 58a; Studio-Annika, 19b; SVproduction, 19a; tilo, 4a; Tom Brakefield, 35a; twildlife, 34; urosr, 21b; Wavebreakmedia Ltd, 46a; yunava1, 41; zanskar, 17a; Zoonar RF, 56; zothen, 7; zysman, 25.

Animal Illustrations: julos/Thinkstock.

We acknowledge the financial support of the Government of Canada.
Nous reconnaissons l'appui financier du gouvernement du Canada.

Funded by the Government of Canada
Financé par le gouvernement du Canada | **Canadä**

Produced with the assistance of the Government of Alberta, Alberta Media Fund.

Alberta
Government

PC: 38